IN THE COMPANY OF STARS GÉRARD UFÉRAS

To my mother

FOREWORD BRIGITTE LEFÈVRE
TEXT GÉRARD MANNONI

IN THE COMPANY OF STARS GÉRARD UFÉRAS

THE PARIS OPERA BALLET

Flammarion

Foreword

For an entire season, Gérard Uféras followed the Ballet de l'Opéra National de Paris (The Paris Opera Ballet). He shadowed the dancers not only in the rehearsal rooms, where the ballet takes shape, and in the wings or backstage, but also on their tour of Japan, training his lens on moments from their daily life generally unseen by the public. With his own artistic sensibility, he unveils places and people entirely free of artifice, leading us where audiences never go but where the artists feel at home: in exercise rooms, each bearing the name of an important figure who has contributed to the glory of the Ballet—such as the studios Lifar, Petipa, Nureyev, Franchetti, and the rotundas Zambelli and Chauviré—but also in the Foyer de la Danse, where the troupe gathers to warm up before each performance. Page after page, Uféras' photographs recall the incessant, arduous, yet often exhilarating toil that rhythms the Company's calendar as the ballet gradually blossoms into splendor. From the wings, he captures the rapt concentration that precedes a dancer's entrance, the glances, gestures, and attitudes, each mirroring an emotion, a moment of effort or repose. There is a whole other life that takes place behind the curtain.

These photographs constitute a tribute to the Company: beyond the troupe, they reveal personalities, a genuine family, where the complicity between the dancers, the ties linking The Paris Opera Ballet School to the corps de ballet, the collaboration between all those involved in the performance can be savored in telling images that the photographer has caught, as it were, on the fly. And so I invite the reader to enter a world bathed in a unique kind of magic, and it is my heartfelt wish that through it he or she should gain insight into the artistic community that makes the Company what it is today.

BRIGITTE LEFÈVRE

Maybe dance is, at the root, an art of contradiction

Sacred in origin, dance was condemned early on by the Church, which nevertheless found a place for it in its sanctuaries. Dance is a source of transitory images which, scarcely embodied, are erased forever. It is as ancient as drawing in the history of humankind and undoubtedly precedes the word, being able, like language, to communicate messages, even political ones. An expression of the body and of sensuality, its aim is immateriality and abstraction. Rooted in a technique forged by strain and pain, outwardly it must convey only ease and facility. In an era when transmission and communication are dominated by machines, it remains an anachronistic, initiatory art, upheld by a society of artists in which masters and apprentices collaborate in a manner more akin to that of the guildsmen of the Middle Ages than to a multinational in the third millennium.

A dance company—whether performing, on tour, backstage, in rehearsal, or at the barre—is a world apart, peopled by beings that seem a mix of butterfly, sex symbol, and athlete; a universe at once very near to and very far from us, whose ingredients are inextricably intertwined on all conscious and unconscious levels. The art of the photographer conveys its life, its breathtaking diversity, capturing and preserving infinitesimal fractions of a second that are in themselves moments of eternity.

As the history of humanity demonstrates, and non-European civilizations remind us, from the outset dance has expressed humankind's will to enter into dialogue with the divine. In the Orient, in Africa, in ancient, even prehistoric cultures, jumping, whirling, or more or less codified gesticulations were always more than simple merrymaking; rather they represented an attempt to induce a trance-like state so as to reach the gods. Temple dancing girls in Asia, Greek bacchantes, the priestesses of ancient Egypt, African medicine men, as well as many others, all functioned as actors or directors of choreographic events that were seen as a path to communication with the gods. The phenomenon was universal, though admittedly less common among the Romans and the Gauls. The hallowed character of dance is even present in the Bible: one merely has to think of King David.

The advent of Christianity might have been expected to be just another phase in the history of these traditions and rites, so the very fact that the contrary was true introduced a further twist to the story. From the beginning of the Christian era, the Church saw fit to condemn and prohibit dancing in what was the opening salvo in the religion's tumultuous, polemic, and constantly changing relationship with the body. Over the centuries, however, this condemnation took on various forms that mirror the history of the faith and of its culture. The astonishing thing is that the Church never actually stopped staging dances of its own. Ornamental initials in books of hours from medieval monasteries show monks holding each other by the little finger in charming roundelays.

By the middle of the sixteenth century, while the terrible Inquisition raged, the corps de ballet of Seville Cathedral pleaded with the pope to lift an interdict preventing them from performing, implying not only that they had previously done so but that the Church acceded to their request.

The friars accompanying the conquistadors to South America were keen to convert local pagan festivals into dance processions that conducted the populace from the public square to the nave of the newly built cathedrals. And there were also *danses macabres* staged at stopping places along pilgrimage routes, while others formed part of the mystery plays danced on cathedral forecourts. In the seventeenth century, too, the Jesuits organized courtly ballets for their novices in some of their colleges. Evolving over time, this doubly ambivalent and singularly complicated relationship between Christianity and dance has continued up to the present day, though no one today is shocked to see choreographed versions of a Bach's Passion or Mozart's Requiem, even if dancing has been abandoned in convents.

Nothing is more transitory than a dance step. It is perpetually "becoming," writ in the sands of time. Scarcely begun, it is already nearly over. A round dance, no matter how rudimentary, dies as soon as it materializes. How long does a given attitude, a *piqué arabesque*, for instance, last? A tenth of a second? And what about a *grand jeté* or a leap that seems to us to hang in the air? Not much longer. A dancer poised in equilibrium for two or three seconds feels like an eternity. Is it all really worth the effort? And yet in our civilization, since it took the form of spectacle this fleeting language—a spontaneous outgrowth that over time has been codified—has served to embody (initially through allegory and later more explicitly) not only hundreds of romantic fables, but also real historical episodes, and in the past it has even managed to convey political statements sufficiently overt to have sparked civil wars or cemented alliances. From La Délivrance de Renaud, aping Louis XIII's coming-of-age, to the Green Table, from Spartacus to The Red Detachment of Women, and any number of Soviet or Chinese productions, this art of the ephemeral has also marked human history in what is a striking contradiction between an art form that evaporates almost as soon as it takes shape and the enduring resonance of the message it seeks to convey and preserve. Even if many of today's choreographers yield to the temptation to have their dancers speak, dance is still basically a language of the body, and thus of sensuality. In many of its sacred forms, it already prepared, heralded, or even represented the union between the physical and the divine.

The motionless body in painting or statuary can never make the impact of one in motion. Often performed naked in ancient rites and then clothed once it became a public affair, and today once more divested of its coverings as more and more performances make use of near or even total nudity, dance inevitably sets up an incarnate and therefore concrete relation between dancer and viewer, a fusion between sensation and imagination.

Moreover, perhaps dance, along with music, is the most immaterial artistic language, the one that best expresses the abstract, conjuring up dreams, encapsulating the ontological dimension of the human. One might even venture that the foremost present-day creators, by exploiting the apparent contradiction of the expressive possibilities of the human body, have shown themselves capable of depicting not only the private angst of contemporary man but also the religious and mythical aspirations that underpinned the most ancient civilizations.

When, in the course of the eighteenth century, dance at last emerged as an autonomous performing art distinct from the opera, it set about stabilizing its codes with increasing rigor and precision. The so-called "classical" technique—a time-honored foundation, even for those intent on subverting, rejecting, or demolishing it—is rooted in a logic of effort. Everyone is aware of the long years of apprenticeship, the daily routine of training, the tough realities of a world in which physical pain is omnipresent in a thousand different ways, where performers have to regulate the body and even overcome it. And all this so that on stage the exact opposite image is given—one of ease, grace, complete effortlessness. Anyone fortunate enough to have been allowed the magical experience of watching a dance performance from the wings knows how the seductive, ethereal creature that the public sees toying with its body and muscles with such disconcerting facility is transformed as soon as it exits between two scenery flats into an exhausted, perspiring, breathless shell, likely to collapse and stretch out on the bare floor before springing off once more toward the footlights with the same buoyancy and energy as before, the patch of damp left behind on the floor the only sign of his or her incredible exertions.

And lastly, it must be admitted that there is an odd contradiction between the cutting-edge advances in communication technology of which dancers are so fond, and for which the world of dance has found a myriad of different uses, and the fundamentally initiatory character of this art, where the direct rapport between master and pupil remains irreplaceable. Dancers are by and large a youthful lot and, as they fly about on their tours of Asia, they cannot resist the most up-to-date contraptions that modern electronics has to offer: cell phones, TVs, PDAs, computers, MP3 players.... Video, too, has assumed an essential role in communicating and preserving repertories, and even in creative choreography. The core programs of the majority of the larger companies are now recorded and released, while many choreographers remodel or create works with film in mind. And of course, many dancers first become interested in the choreography of a repertory ballet by watching a performance on screen. Yet any given interpretation or creation is always forged through direct contact between master, or choreographer, and dancer. Nothing can replace it: the precise movement to be reproduced, and which can only be demonstrated by someone who knows exactly what is required; the hand that adjusts the position of an arm or a head to the nearest millimeter; a word of reprimand or encouragement; the authority of a celebrated mentor whose art perhaps inspired the same dancer's vocation. The ballet, therefore, is a world of unmediated contact between human beings, physical as well as psychological, where mysterious impulses flow from one body to another, where the sensitivity of one artist meshes with that of another, a place where a wealth of experience is passed on to minds with an insatiable thirst for knowledge—quite at odds with relationships or interchange based on text messaging, e-mailing, or an image on the screen.

How, then, is a photographer supposed to capture an art and a world that are by nature so full of contradiction? High-speed film would certainly be useful to capture that split-second leap or step that attains perfection, and can yield beautiful results, too. Or, in the quest for the opposite effect, an impressionistic blur that seeks to convey the fluidity of a movement might effectively portray the ambiance of a work or scene. And perhaps by deploying elaborate lighting that sculpts the dancer's body like Michelangelo's chisel, an interesting tribute could be provided to one of the most impressive aspects of the ballet. But however rewarding these approaches may be, they cannot account for the complexity of an art whose manifold contradictions have been outlined above.

For the photographer intent on conveying this inner complexity as truthfully as possible, a preferable option is perhaps to endeavor to record (according to his personal sensitivities and without preconceptions) the countless moments that make up the life of a company—at work, on stage, or on tour, straining at the leash or unwinding, as individuals or in a group—breaking each movement down into its components, or framing a particular part of the body that suddenly appears marked by a graceful position or by a certain lighting, ornament, or costume. Neither catalog nor balance sheet, the photographer's work has to tread the line between sensation and imagination, concrete and abstract, past and present, sacred and profane. The challenge is immense and calls for as much instinct as patience, as much spontaneity as expertise. But whoever rises to it knows that he, too, has gained entrance into that magic circle where, since the hallowed festivals of prehistory, the soul of dance is to be found.

GÉRARD MANNONI

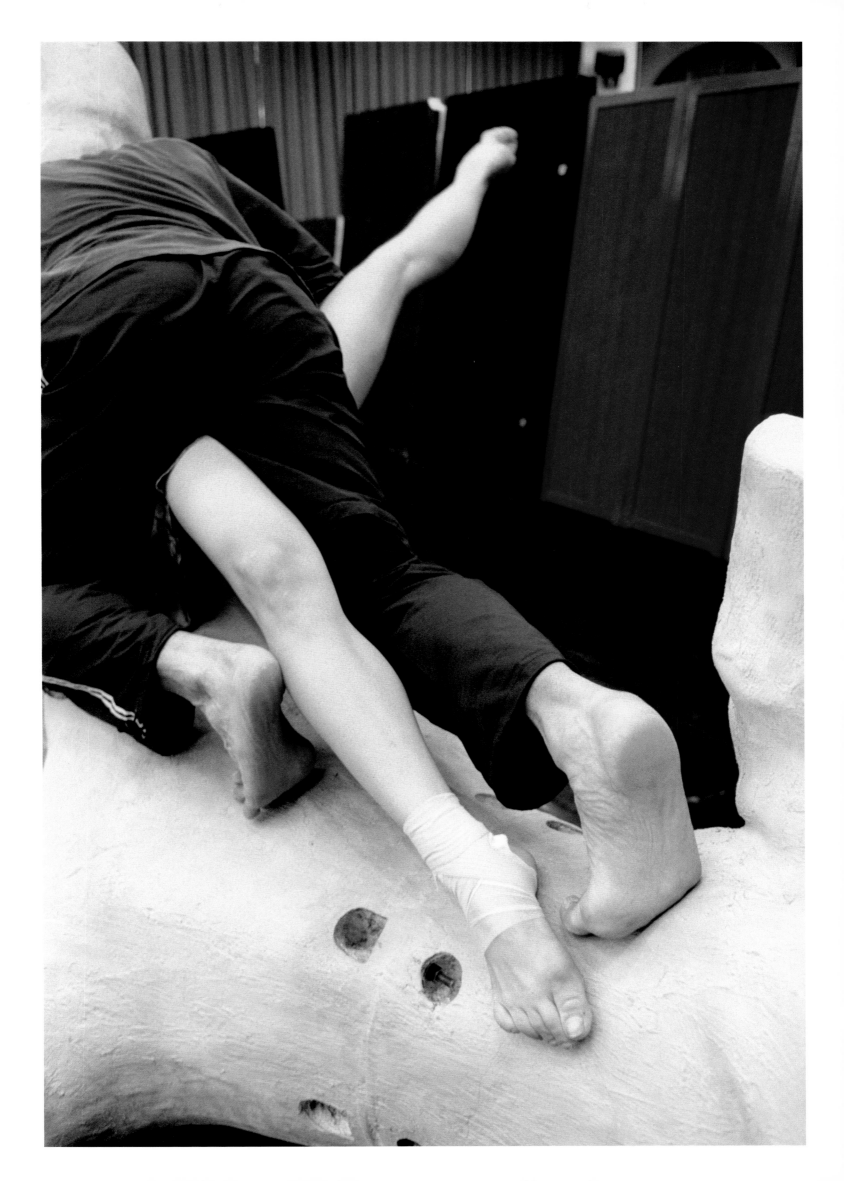

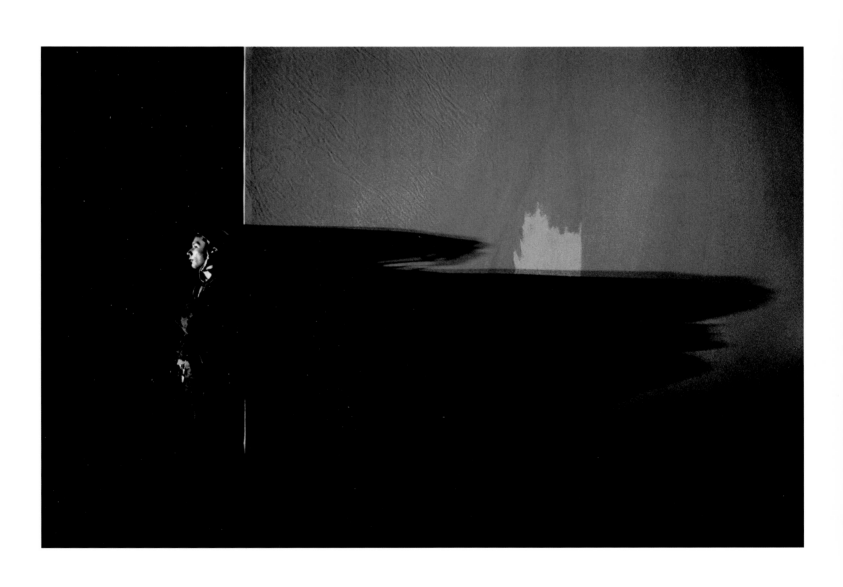

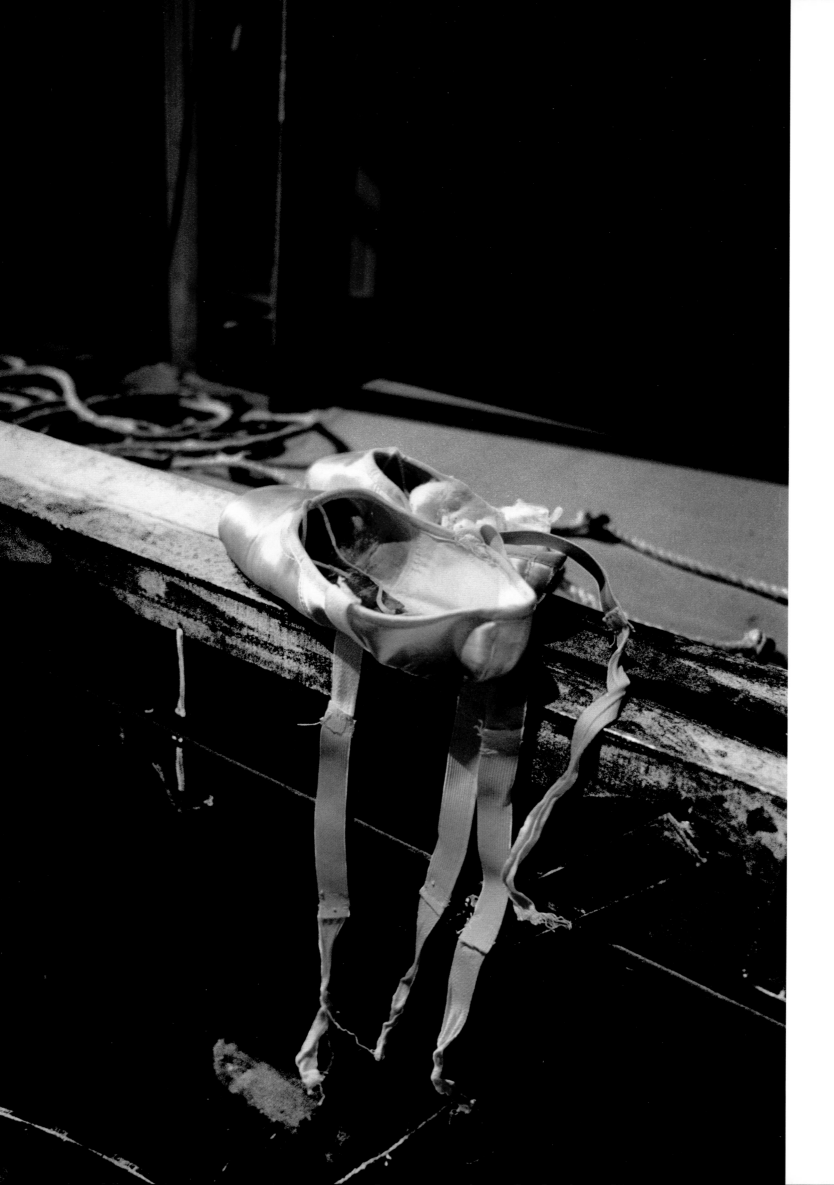

In the wings during Rudolf Nureyev's *Sleeping Beauty*, December 2004.

Back to the dressing rooms after the curtain calls, performance by The Paris Opera Ballet School, Palais Garnier, December 2004.

Alexandra Cardinale in the Foyer de la Danse before a performance of *Serenade* by George Balanchine, November 2003.

The Paris Opera Ballet School, Nanterre, November 2003.

Études by Harald Lander, September 2004.

Martin Chaix and Alexandra Cardinale rehearsing the dance of the cats in Rudolf Nureyev's *Sleeping Beauty*, October 2004.

The Paris Opera Ballet School, Nanterre, November 2003.

Nathalie Aubin in *Pas./Parts* by William Forsythe, December 2004.
Jean-Philippe Dury and Juliette Gernez in *Pas./Parts* by William Forsythe, December 2004.

Kader Belarbi in Pina Bausch's *Orpheus and Eurydice*, June 2005.
Eleonora Abbagnato and Jérémie Bélingard rehearsing *Le Jeune Homme et la Mort* by Roland Petit, June 2005.

During a rehearsal of Pina Bausch's *Orpheus and Eurydice*, May 2005.
Laëtitia Pujol in *Wuthering Heights* by Kader Belarbi, March 2005.

Stéphane Phavorin before a rehearsal of Pina Bausch's *Orpheus and Eurydice*, May 2005.
Sabrina Mallem before the performance of *Pas./Parts* by William Forsythe, December 2004.

Alice Renavand in the Foyer de la Danse before the performance of Pina Bausch's *Orpheus and Eurydice*, May 2005.
Émilie Cozette talking to Elena Bonnay before the Concours Annuel that appointed her *première danseuse*, December 2004.

Rehearsal of *Wuthering Heights* by Kader Belarbi, February 2005.
Rehearsal of Angelin Preljocaj's *Medea*, October 2004.

Natacha Quernet backstage during Rudolf Nureyev's *Sleeping Beauty*, December 2004.
Laurène Levy and Laura Hecquet, dress rehearsal of Rudolf Nureyev's *Sleeping Beauty*, November 2004.

Eleonora Abbagnato and Jérémie Bélingard in *Pas./Parts* by William Forsythe, December 2004.

Stéphanie Romberg in Rudolf Nureyev's *Sleeping Beauty*, November 2004.
Eleonora Abbagnato and Wilfried Romoli in Angelin Preljocaj's *Medea*, November 2004.

Agnès Letestu and Laurent Hilaire rehearsing *Serenade* by George Balanchine, November 2003.
The Paris Opera Ballet School, Nanterre, November 2003.

Nicolas Le Riche and Eleonora Abbagnato rehearsing Kader Belarbi's *Wuthering Heights*, February 2005.

Laurène Levy and Audric Bezard in an elevator at the Opéra Bastille, November 2004.

Charlotte Ranson in Pina Bausch's *Orpheus and Eurydice*, June 2005.
Nicolas Paul warming up before a performance of *Signes* by Carolyn Carlson, Japan tour, Nagano, April 2005.

Laurence Laffon in Trisha Brown's *Glacial Decoy*, December 2004.
Laure Muret and Stéphane Elizabé in Rudolf Nureyev's *Sleeping Beauty*, November 2004.

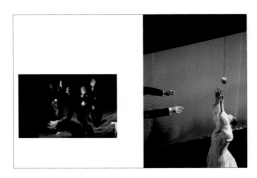

Dorothée Gilbert in Pina Bausch's *Orpheus and Eurydice*, June 2005.
Émilie Cozette and Stéphane Phavorin in Pina Bausch's *Orpheus and Eurydice*, June 2005.

Glass Pieces by Jerome Robbins, September 2004.
José Martinez in John Neumeyer's *Sylvia*, March 2005.

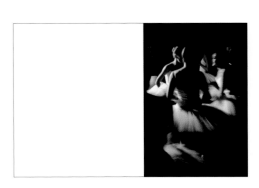

Études by Harald Lander, October 2004.

Dorothée Gilbert and Sabrina Mallem in
Pas./Parts by William Forsythe, December 2004.

Lionel Delanoë rehearsing Adrien Couvez for
the Concours Annuel, December 2004.
Muriel Hallé's hands in a rehearsal of Rudolf
Nureyev's *Sleeping Beauty*, November 2004.

The Paris Opera Ballet School, Nanterre,
November 2003.

Performance by The Paris Opera Ballet School,
José Martinez's *Scaramouche*, costumes by
Agnès Letestu, Palais Garnier, March 2005.
Mathilde Froustey in *Études* by Harald Lander,
October 2004.

Performance by The Paris Opera Ballet School,
José Martinez's *Scaramouche*, costumes by
Agnès Letestu, Palais Garnier, March 2005.

Backstage during the performance by The Paris
Opera Ballet School of José Martinez's
Scaramouche, costumes by Agnès Letestu,
Palais Garnier, March 2005.
Backstage before a performance of John
Neumeyer's *Sylvia*, March 2005.

Marie-Solène Boulet and Émilie Cozette backs-
tage during Rudolf Nureyev's *Sleeping Beauty*,
December 2004.
Kader Belarbi and Séverine Westermann
backstage during Carolyn Carlson's *Signes*,
Japan tour, Nagano, April 2005.

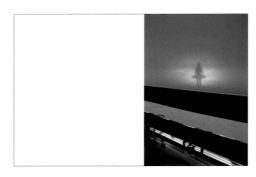

Marie-Isabelle Peracchi at the Concours Annuel,
December 2004.

Rehearsal of Rudolf Nureyev's *Sleeping Beauty*,
November 2004.
Charlotte Ranson backstage during Rudolf
Nureyev's *Sleeping Beauty*, December 2004.

Sleeping Beauty by Rudolf Nureyev,
December 2004.

Études by Harald Lander, September 2004.
Les Familiers du labyrinthe by Michèle Noiret,
February 2005.

The Seven Deadly Sins by Laura Scozzi,
February 2005.
Backstage during *Les Familiers du labyrinthe*
by Michèle Noiret, February 2005.

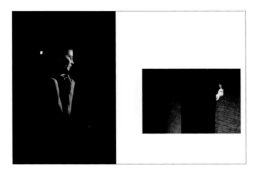

Marie-Agnès Gillot backstage during Angelin Preljocaj's *Medea*, November 2004.
Kader Belarbi in Francine Lancelot's *Bach Suite*, December 2004.

Miho Fujii backstage during Rudolf Nureyev's *Cinderella*, May 2005.
Laëtitia Pujol and Delphine Moussin in *Sylvia* by John Neumeyer, March 2005.

Backstage during Rudolf Nureyev's *Sleeping Beauty*, December 2004.

Mathilde Froustey and Alexandre Labrot backstage during rehearsals for Rudolf Nureyev's *Sleeping Beauty*, November 2004.
Back from the Japan tour, Nagano, April 2005.

Malin Thoors rehearsing Vanessa Legassy in Rudolf Nureyev's *Sleeping Beauty*, November 2004.
Rehearsal of Rudolf Nureyev's *Sleeping Beauty*, November 2004.

Jérémie Bélingard in the Foyer de la Danse, December 2004.
José Martinez in Rudolf Nureyev's *Sleeping Beauty*, December 2004.

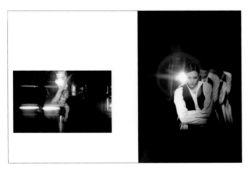

Marie-Agnès Gillot in Angelin Preljocaj's *Medea*, November 2004.
Séverine Westermann in Carolyn Carlson's *Signes*, Japan tour, Nagano, April 2005.

Kader Belarbi, December 2004.
Jean-Guillaume Bart in Rudolf Nureyev's *Sleeping Beauty*, November 2004.

Paris Opera Ballet School, Nanterre, November 2003.

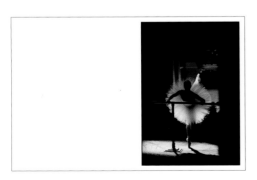

Sandrine Marache in Harald Lander's *Études*, September 2004.

Jean-Philippe Dury's shadow, May 2005.
Backstage during *Signes* by Carolyn Carlson, Japan tour, Nagano, April 2005.

Laurène Levy, Julie Martel, and Marie-Solène Boulet in Harald Lander's *Études*, September 2004.
Backstage during Rudolf Nureyev's *Sleeping Beauty*, December 2004.

Alice Renavand backstage during *Signes*
by Carolyn Carlson, Japan tour, Nagano,
April 2005.

Nicolas Le Riche and Eleonora Abbagnato,
rehearsal of Kader Belarbi's *Wuthering Heights*,
February 2005.
Rehearsing Kader Belarbi's *Wuthering Heights*,
February 2005.

Break during the rehearsal of Rudolf Nureyev's
Sleeping Beauty, Julien Meyzindi and Peggy
Dursort, October 2004.
Charlotte Ranson and Nicolas Paul during a
break at the Noureyev studio, May 2005.

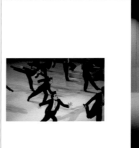

The Paris Opera Ballet School, Nanterre,
November 2003.
Eleonora Abbagnato in the Foyer de la Danse
before a performance of *Afternoon of a Faun*
by Jerome Robbins, November 2003.

The Seven Deadly Sins by Laura Scozzi,
February 2005.
Nicolas Paul, Bruno Bouché, Vincent Chaillet
before a performance of Carolyn Carlson's
Signes, Japan tour, Nagano, April 2005.

John Neumeyer's *Sylvia*, March 2005.
Opéra Bastille, March 2005.

Aurélia Bellet and Jean-Christophe Guerri in
Carolyn Carlson's *Signes*, Japan tour, Nagano,
April 2005.

Études by Harald Lander, October 2004.

Nicolas Le Riche in John Neumeyer's *Sylvia*,
March 2005.
Géraldine Wiart in Trisha Brown's *Glacial Decoy*,
December 2004.

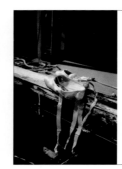

Caroline Robert, Gwenaëlle Vauthier, Pascal
Aubin, and Christine Peltzer, before Rudolf
Nureyev's *Sleeping Beauty*, November 2004.
Backstage during Rudolf Nureyev's *Sleeping
Beauty*, December 2004.

Laura Hecquet's ballet shoes backstage during
Rudolf Nureyev's *Sleeping Beauty*,
December 2004.
Rehearsal of Rudolf Nureyev's *Sleeping Beauty*,
November 2004.

Karine Averty, Mélanie Hurel, Emmanuel
Thibault rehearsing Rudolf Nureyev's
Cinderella, February 2005.
Aurélien Houette at the Concours Annuel,
December 2004.

Stéphanie Romberg and Yann Saïz rehearsing
John Neumeyer's *Sylvia*, February 2005.
Rehearsing Rudolf Nureyev's *Sleeping Beauty*,
November 2004.

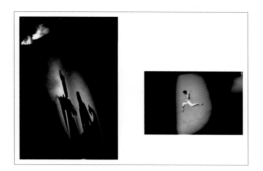

Sleeping Beauty by Rudolf Nureyev,
December 2004.
Nicolas Le Riche in John Neumeyer's *Sylvia*,
March 2005.

Les Familiers du labyrinthe by Michèle Noiret,
February 2005.

Mélanie Hurel in *Ich bin...* by Suzanne Linke,
February 2005.

Alice Renavand, dress rehearsal of Pina
Bausch's *Orpheus and Eurydice*, May 2005.
Marie-Agnès Gillot and Nicolas Le Riche in
Kader Belarbi's *Wuthering Heights*, March 2005.

During the Concours Annuel, December 2004.
Caroline Bance watching *Glacial Decoy*
by Trisha Brown from the wings, December 2004.

Orpheus and Eurydice by Pina Bausch,
June 2005.

Vanessa Legassy backstage during Harald
Lander's *Études*, October 2004.
Aubane Philbert backstage during Harald
Lander's *Études*, October 2004.

Aurélia Bellet backstage during Trisha Brown's
Glacial Decoy, December 2004.
Christelle Granier in Pina Bausch's *Orpheus and
Eurydice*, June 2005.

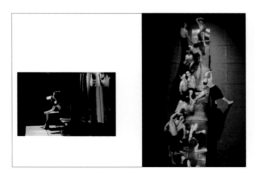

Jean-Philippe Dury backstage during Carolyn
Carlson's *Signes*, Japan tour, Nagano, April 2005.
MC 14/22 "ceci est mon corps" by Angelin
Preljocaj, November 2004.

Lucie Mateci during the Concours Annuel,
December 2004.

Christelle Granier backstage during *Études*
by Harald Lander, September 2004.
Elizabeth Maurin's farewell at the Opéra Bastille
following her performance in Rudolf Nureyev's
Romeo and Juliet, June 29, 2005.

Acknowledgments

The book you hold in your hands represents what will remain for me one of the most rewarding experiences in my life as a photographer. When I sauntered through the stage door of the Palais Garnier to shoot a magazine article on The Paris Opera Ballet, I never thought that the adventure would last some three years, that it would culminate in a book and bring me not only a sense of wonder but also many priceless friendships. Yet people had often mentioned The Paris Opera Ballet to me on my travels, and from Moscow to Havana its reputation is a byword for excellence. But to have witnessed the same passionate commitment to this profession and art in the eight-year-old dancers at the ballet school and the most polished *étoile* alike is a rare honor indeed, especially when such intensity is accompanied by the modesty of individuals who are all too aware that their art will be outlived, and that no career can be guaranteed to last forever.

Of course, I encountered this determination coupled with an enormous love for dance among the dancers themselves, but also, and to no less a degree, among the professors, *repetiteurs*, ballet masters, pianists, regisseurs, costumiers, dressers, makeup artists, hairstylists, stagehands, to name but a few, and this every day and at every evening's performance, for The Paris Opera Ballet is a place where the work is unstinting. Indeed, it was sometimes hard to keep up with the Company, but my efforts were always rewarded by encounters with such inquisitive, enthusiastic people. The Paris Opera Ballet is not a citadel dedicated to preserving its heritage in aspic; it embraces the world of today, and welcomes contemporary creations that question the role of man in present-day society and which keep this venerable house both on its toes and avid for more.

This adventure would never have been possible without the support of Gérard Mortier, who once again afforded me his trust; nor without Brigitte Lefèvre, Director of The Paris Opera Ballet, an exceptional institution that many other capital cities can only dream of.

A thank-you to the dancers, or rather I should say my dancer friends, since they welcomed me with open arms and let me share in their everyday existence with unflagging generosity; I thank them for their art that so often dazzled me and for their kindness. And thank you also to all the people in dance and theater who make the Opéra National de Paris such a magical place.

I wish to express my gratitude to all those whose aid and advice helped me materialize a project that has meant so much to me: Jodi Bieber, Jean-Louis Bouchard, Guy Bourreau, Kristina Briaudeau, Jean-François Camp, Nathalie Charon, Livia Corbo, Lorraine Dauchez, Hélène Millara Deron, Francine Deroudille, Jean-François Dessain, Marie Dorigny, Hani Gresh, Mary Guerga, Isabelle Hoppenot, Brigitte Huard, Jean-Yves Kaced, Martine Kahane, Alain Mingam, Jean-Luc Monterosso, Grazia Neri, Baodine Nguyen, Willy Ronis, Cindy Schifano, Marie Hélène and Jean-Marie Smiejan, Emmanuelle Soulat, Vera Soulier, Gaia Tripoli, Tom and Fanny Uféras, Vincent Vachette, Jean-Pierre Vallin, François Vessière, and Stéphane Wargnier.

Thank you to my agencies: Rapho (Paris) and Grazia Neri (Milan).

I also wish to thank Kodak Pathé (France) for image production, the Dupon laboratory, the Opéra National de Paris, as well as Econocom SA, Epson France, and the Maison Européenne de la Photographie for staging the exhibition.

Biography

Gérard Uféras, who is represented by the Rapho and Grazia Neri agencies, was born and lives in Paris. In 1984, he began a regular collaboration with the French daily *Libération*, for which he undertook numerous reportages and which organized his debut exhibition. He has since become a frequent contributor to *Télérama*, *Time*, *Beaux-Arts*, *The Independent Magazine*, *The New York Times*, *Jardin des modes*, *Das Magazin*, *Lo Specchio della Stampa*, *Marie-Claire* (Italy), *Marie-Claire* (France), *Madame Figaro*, *Le Monde*, *View Point*, *L'Officiel*, *L'Express*, *Io Donna*, *D: La Repubblica Delle Donne*, *Amica*, *Il Corriere della Sera*, among others.

He helped to set up the Vu agency in 1986, and since 1993 he has been a member of the Rapho agency. Alongside his career in photojournalism, he also works as a portraitist, undertakes advertising campaigns and fashion shoots, and pursues his own personal projects that have culminated in exhibitions in various countries. He has received a host of awards for his work, which appears in collections at the Maison Européenne de la Photographie in Paris, the Union Centrale des Arts Décoratifs, the Bibliothèque Nationale de France, the National Gallery in London, the Musée de l'Élysée in Lausanne, the House of Photography in Moscow, at the Salzburg Festival, and in the Fonds National d'art contemporain, and the Henkel Collection in Germany.

EXHIBITIONS

1984	Galerie Libération/La Chambre claire, Paris
1986	"Photographes en quête d'auteurs," Direction du Livre, Paris
1988	"Regards sur le Palais Garnier," Mois de la Photo, Paris
1988	"Lectures, lectures," BPI/Centre Pompidou, Paris
1988	"Voir la Suisse autrement," Musée de l'Élysée, Lausanne
1992	"Glyndebourne, un jardin d'Opéra," Galerie Orcofi, Paris
1993	Musée de l'Élysée, Lausanne
1996	"The Visit," Ramsgate
1996	French Institute, Bratislava
1997	Jahrhunderthalle, Frankfurt
1997	Carrousel du Louvre
1997	Salzburg Festival
2000	"Eleganza momenti rubati," Galleria Grazia Neri, Milan Galleria Battistoni, Rome
2000	"Haute Couture," Harrod's, London
2000	"Hand Mode," Web bar, Paris
2001	"L'Étoffe des rêves," Union centrale des arts décoratifs, Paris
2001	Grand Manège, International Fashion Festival, Moscow
2002	Bunkamura Gallery, Tokyo
2002	Musée de l'Élysée, Lausanne
2003	Petrovsky passage, Moscow
2004	Bibliothèque nationale de France, Library and Museum of the Opera, Paris
2006	"Lumières d'Etoiles," Festival L'œil en Seyne, La Seyne-sur-Mer

PRIZES

1987	Art Directors' Prize
1990	Prix Villa Médicis hors les murs
1991	BP Arts Journalism Award
1997	World Press Photo
1999	Grand Prix SCAM

BIBLIOGRAPHY

Mezcal. Paris: Plume, 1993.
The Visit. Maidstone: Photoworks, 1996.
Opera. Heidelberg: Braus, 1997.
Il Piccolo Teatro di Milano. Milan: Mondadori, 1997.
L'Étoffe des rêves. Paris: Éditions du Collectionneur, 2001.
Un fantôme à l'Opéra. Paris: Éditions du Collectionneur, 2003.
Les coulisses du festival. Paris: Flammarion, 2005.
Saint Gobain PAM 150 ans. France, 2006 (published internally).

Translated from the French by David Radzinowicz
Copyediting: Helen Adedotun
Design: www.monsieurtom.com
Color Separation: Les Artisans du Regard, Paris

Photography © Gérard Uféras/Rapho
www.gerarduferas.com

This book was printed with the support of **Hermès** as well as **AROP, UFF**, and **Condat**.
Printed on 170 g/m² Condat silk offset paper

Distributed in North America by Rizzoli International Publications, Inc.

Simultaneously published in French as *Un pas vers les étoiles*
© Flammarion, Paris, 2006

English-language edition
© Flammarion, Paris, 2006

www.editions.flammarion.com

06 07 08 4 3 2 1
ISBN-10: 2-0803-0000-8
ISBN-13: 978-2-08-030000-3
Dépôt légal: 11/2006

Printed in France by Le Govic